YOUR ANCIENT
ROME

Homework Helper

by *Colin Hynson*
Consultant: Dr. Isabella Sandwell

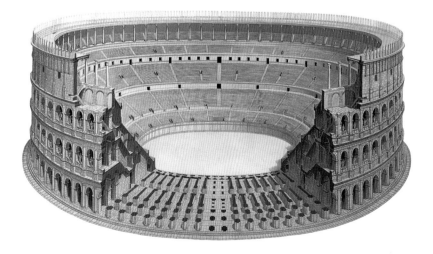

ticktock
M E D I A

How to use this book

Each topic in this book is clearly labelled and contains all these components:

Topic heading

Introduction to the topic

Sub-topic 1 offers complete information about one aspect of the topic

Choose a word from the Keyword Contents on page 3. Then, turn to the correct page and look for your word in BOLD CAPITALS. This will take you straight to the information you need

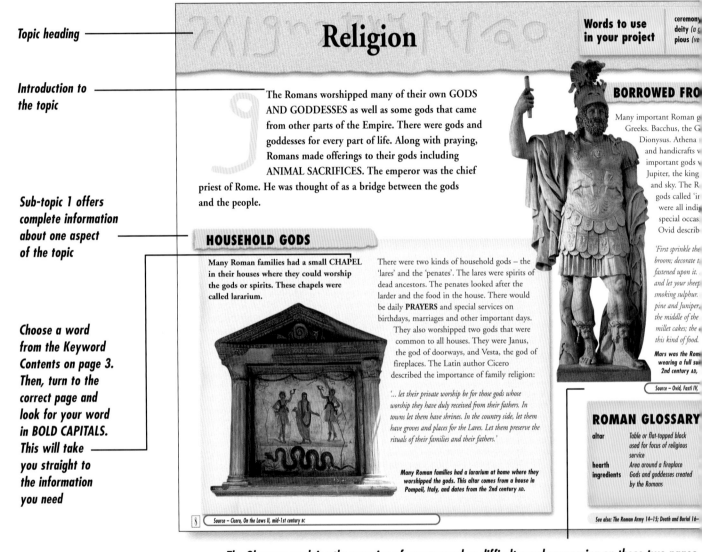

Religion

Words to use in your project

ceremony
deity (a g
pious (ve

The Romans worshipped many of their own GODS AND GODDESSES as well as some gods that came from other parts of the Empire. There were gods and goddesses for every part of life. Along with praying, Romans made offerings to their gods including ANIMAL SACRIFICES. The emperor was the chief priest of Rome. He was thought of as a bridge between the gods and the people.

BORROWED FRO

Many important Roman g
Greeks. Bacchus, the G
Dionysus. Athena
and handicrafts v
important gods v
Jupiter, the king
and sky. The R
gods called 'ir
were all indig
special occas
Ovid describ

*'First sprinkle the
broom; decorate t
fastened upon it.
and let your sheep
smoking sulphur.
pine and Juniper,
the middle of the
millet cakes; the
this kind of food.*

**Mars was the Rom
wearing a full sui
2nd century AD,**

Source – Ovid, Fasti IV,

HOUSEHOLD GODS

Many Roman families had a small CHAPEL in their houses where they could worship the gods or spirits. These chapels were called lararium.

There were two kinds of household gods – the 'lares' and the 'penates'. The lares were spirits of dead ancestors. The penates looked after the larder and the food in the house. There would be daily **PRAYERS** and special services on birthdays, marriages and other important days. They also worshipped two gods that were common to all houses. They were Janus, the god of doorways, and Vesta, the god of fireplaces. The Latin author Cicero described the importance of family religion:

'... let their private worship be for those gods whose worship they have duly received from their fathers. In towns let them have shrines. In the country side, let them have groves and places for the Lares. Let them preserve the rituals of their families and their fathers.'

Many Roman families had a lararium at home where they worshipped the gods. This altar comes from a house in Pompeii, Italy, and dates from the 2nd century AD.

ROMAN GLOSSARY

altar	Table or flat-topped block used for focus of religious service
hearth	Area around a fireplace
ingredients	Gods and goddesses created by the Romans

Source – Cicero, On the Laws II, mid-1st century BC

8

See also: The Roman Army 14–15; Death and Burial 16–

The Glossary explains the meaning of any unusual or difficult words appearing on these two pages

Copyright © *ticktock* Entertainment Ltd 2004

First published in Great Britain in 2004 by *ticktock* Media Ltd.,

Unit 2, Orchard Business Centre, North Farm Road, Tunbridge Wells, Kent, TN2 3XF

We would like to thank: Egan-Reid Ltd for their help with this book.

ISBN 1 86007 540 1 HB

ISBN 1 86007 534 7 PB

Printed in China

A CIP catalogue record for this book is available from the British Library.

Sub-topic 2 offers complete information about one aspect of the topic

Keyword Contents

Some suggested words to use in your project

The Case Study is a closer look at a famous person, artefact or building that relates to the topic

polytheism (believing in and worshipping many gods)

sacrifice (something killed as an offering to a god)

rites (rituals)

EKS

from the
as renamed
f wisdom
a. The most
of war; and
d of the light
e original
a and Saturn
rovided
gods. The poet
Paralia festival:

sweep it with a
nd branches
are sulphur,
d by the
e olive trees,
nd crackle in
illet with the
al pleasure in

y shown
ates from the

for storing food
house where
ould worship
e for worshipping
acred person
created for worship

80–31

CASE STUDY

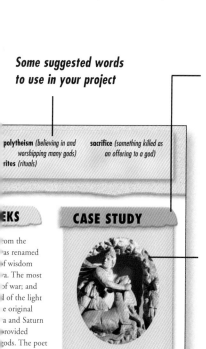

Each photo or illustration is described and discussed in its accompanying text

The god Mithras was very popular with soldiers because they believed it conquered darkness and disorder. This relief comes from Rome and dates from the 3rd century AD.

The God Mithras

One of the most important gods for the Roman army was Mithras, the god of light and the sun. The sun god Mithras was originally worshipped by the Persians who lived in what is now modern Iran. It reached Rome in the 1st century AD. It appealed to the army because as the god of light, Mithras conquered darkness and disorder. An inscription from Germany shows the dedication of an altar to Mithras:

'In honour of the imperial house, to the unconquerable god mithras the altar was established as result of a vow to the god at their own expense by Aulus Gratius Iuvenis Father of the rites (of Mithras) and Aulus Gratius Potens, soldier of the XXII legion.'

Captions clearly explain what is in the picture

Source – German inscription, AD 236   9

Other pages in the book that relate to what you have read here are listed in this bar

At the bottom of each section, a reference bar tells you where the quote has come from

Creation of the Roman Empire

The Italian city of Rome was once ruled by KINGS. In 509 BC, King Tarquin the Proud was driven out of the city and Rome became a REPUBLIC. From then on, Rome began to overpower and rule its neighbours. The Roman Empire soon grew across Europe, North Africa and Asia. Today, taking a country by force would be seen as wrong but the Romans believed they were bringing CIVILISATION to barbarians.

WHERE WAS THE ROMAN EMPIRE?

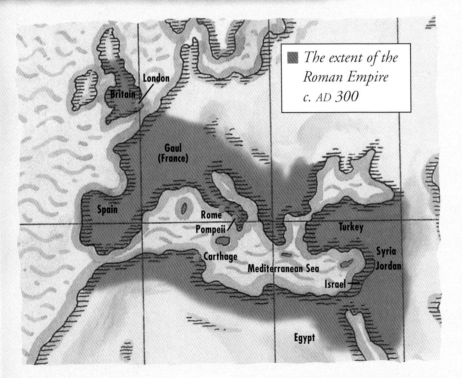

The extent of the Roman Empire c. AD 300

London
Britain
Gaul (France)
Spain
Rome
Pompeii
Carthage
Mediterranean Sea
Turkey
Syria
Jordan
Israel
Egypt

This MAP shows the height of the Roman Empire, under Emperor Trajan, in the 2nd century AD.

This included Spain in 197 BC, and Gaul (modern France), Turkey, Syria, Egypt, Israel and Jordan between 58 and 50 BC. Roman writers such as Herodian and Cassius Dio described the military problems and corruption of the later empire:

'What was the use of destroying barbarians, when the killing in Rome itself and the provinces subject to her was on a larger scale? What was the use of seizing booty from the enemy only to be stripped naked oneself and see one's relatives deprived of their property? An invitation had been given to informers to do their dastardly work with complete license.'

Soon after becaming a Republic, Rome took control of Italy and the Mediterranean. A few hundred years later, the Romans began to CONQUER other lands.

Source – Herodian, History of the Emporers, VII.iii.1, 3rd century AD

WHEN DID THE ROMAN EMPIRE EXIST?

The twin brothers Romulus and Remus founded the city of Rome. This carving dates from the 2nd century AD.

the twin brothers, Romulus and Remus. They were the sons of Mars, the god of war. When they were babies, their uncle put them in the River Tiber to drown but they were rescued and nursed by a wolf. When they grew up, they killed their uncle and built the city of Rome. The author Cicero described Rome's beginnings:

'Consequently it seems to me that Romulus must at the very beginning have had a divine intimation that the city would one day be the seat and hearthstone of a mighty empire; for scarcely could a city placed upon any other site in Italy have more easily maintained our present widespread dominion.'

According to Roman mythology, Rome was founded in 753 BC by

Source – Cicero, On the Republic, vol. V, mid-1st century BC

Creation of the Roman Empire Glossary

booty	Treasure		*(rather than a king)*
barbarians	People without structured society	Empire	Many states ruled over by
corruption	Dishonest actions in return		a single state or king
	for money or personal gain	founded	Built or started something
dastardly	Wicked and cruel	mythology	Stories or beliefs
divine		Republic	A country that is ruled by a small
intimation	Religious/psychic vision		group rather than one person
dominion	A land ruled by its own people	sovereignty	Supreme power or authority

See also: Rulers and Ruled 6–7; Travel and Trade 12–13; The Roman Army 14–15; Buildings and Engineering 18–19

This bronze bust of Claudius is from the 1st century AD.

Conquering Britain

Britain became part of the Roman world in 55 BC when Caesar landed a Roman army on the coast of Kent. It was not until about 100 years later that the Romans **INVADED** Britain again. In the spring of 43 AD, Emperor Claudius arrived in Britain to lead his troops into Colchester. It took another 35 years before Britain was finally conquered and became part of the Roman Empire. An inscription from Rome records the victory of Claudius over Britain and praises him because:

'... he received the surrender of eleven kings of Britain conquered without reverse and because he was the first to subject to the sovereignty of the Roman people barbarian tribes across the ocean.'

Source – Corpus Inscriptionum Latinarum, vol VI no. 920, mid-1st century AD

Rulers and Ruled

At the top of Roman society was the emperor. Next were the 'consuls' who managed the senate and the Roman armies and 'senators' who made the laws. Ordinary people were divided into citizens and non-citizens. CITIZENS had certain rights and privileges that were denied to non-citizens. At the bottom of Roman society were the SLAVES who had no rights at all.

BREAKING THE LAW

In the early days of Rome, the 12 Tables were created. These provided the basis for law and order over the next 1,000 years. If anybody was suspected of breaking the law then they had to face the local judge or 'praetor'.

The praetors were accompanied by two lictors. A lictor would carry an axe tied around a bundle of rods on his shoulder (known as the 'fasces'). The fasces symbolised the praetor's right to **PUNISH** and put to death anybody who was found guilty of a crime. The most powerful praetors were the governors of the various parts of the Roman Empire. Only the emperor was more powerful than them. Roman officials were described by many writers of the period as corrupt. This corruption is suggested in a passage from one of Juvenal's *Satires*:

'When at last the province to which you have long looked forward receives you as governor, put a rein and curb on your anger, and on your greed; take some pity on the poor provincials, keep in mind what the law prescribes, what the senate lies down.'

This 1st century bronze figurine shows a lictor carrying the fasces.

Source – Juvenal Satire 8.88-91, late-1st–early-2nd century BC

Words to use in your project

assassinated (killed)	**democracy** (state where citizens have a say)
corruption (dishonest or illegal behaviour)	**erupted** (broke out)

magistrate (judge)
ruthless (having no pity)
stability (not easily changed)

ROME'S LAWMAKERS

The senate was a group that represented the people of Rome because the members were elected by Roman citizens. The senate was responsible for making **LAWS**. Before the Romans had emperors the senate was the most important organisation in the Empire. Under the emperors it was reduced to just advising the emperor and also as a court of law.

Authors such as Tacitus write about the way the senators flattered the emperor. One writer, Tiberius, even described them as: *'men fit to be slaves'*, meaning that

This detail from an Italian coffin made in 270 AD shows members of the Roman senate.

they grovelled around the emperors in the way slaves served their masters.

Source – Tacitus Annals III.64, late-1st century AD

Rulers and Ruled Glossary

consuls	The top Roman magistrates		of the Empire
curb	Hold back	**senate**	An assembly of important
fasces	A symbol of Roman law and authority		Romans who made laws and advised the rulers of Rome
praetor	A Roman magistrate	**rein**	Restraint – as for a horse
prescribes	Asks or recommends	**senators**	Men elected by citizens to
provincials	People who live in states		join the senate

See also: Creation of the Empire 4–5; Writing 10–11; The Roman Army 14–15; Gladiators 20–21

CASE STUDY

This marble statue of Emperor Augustus was made around 63 BC and comes from Vellentri, Italy.

Emporer Augustus

The Roman Empire was not always ruled by **EMPERORS**. For hundreds of years it was a Republic, governed by generals who fought each other for control. One general named **JULIUS CAESAR** ruled Rome for some time but he was murdered in 44 BC. Caeser's adopted son, Augustus, restored order and was declared the first Emperor of Rome in 27 BC. He ruled until his death in 14 AD. People thought him a wise ruler who brought good things to the people of Rome. The Emperor wrote about his own deeds in what was called the 'Res Gestae'. This boastful document describes:

'The achievements of the divine Augustus by which he brought the world under the empire of the Roman people and the expenses which he bore for the state and people of Rome.'

Source – Augustus, Res Gestae, end-1st century BC

Religion

The Romans worshipped many of their own GODS AND GODDESSES as well as some that came from other parts of the Empire. There were gods and goddesses for every part of life. Along with praying, Romans made offerings to their gods including ANIMAL SACRIFICES. The emperor was the chief priest of Rome. He was thought of as a bridge between the gods and the people.

HOUSEHOLD GODS

Many Roman families had a small CHAPEL in their houses where they could worship the gods or spirits. These chapels were called lararium.

There were two kinds of household gods – the 'lares' and the 'penates'. The lares were spirits of dead ancestors. The penates looked after the larder and the food in the house. There would be daily **PRAYERS** and special services on birthdays, marriages and other important days.

They also worshipped two gods that were common to all houses. They were Janus, the god of doorways, and Vesta, the god of fireplaces. The Latin author Cicero described the importance of family religion:

'... let their private worship be for those gods whose worship they have duly received from their fathers. In towns let them have shrines. In the country side, let them have groves and places for the Lares. Let them preserve the rituals of their families and their fathers.'

Many Roman families had a lararium at home where they worshipped the gods. This altar comes from a house in Pompeii, Italy, and dates from the 2nd century AD.

Source – Cicero, On the Laws II, mid-1st century BC

Words to use in your project

ceremony (important event)	like the gods)
deity (god or goddess)	pious (very religious)
immortal (live forever –	polytheism (believing in and

worshipping many gods)
sacrifice (something killed as an offering to a god)

BORROWED FROM THE GREEKS

Many important Roman gods were adopted from the Greeks. Bacchus, the Greek god of wine, was renamed Dionysus. Athena the Greek goddess of wisdom and handicrafts was renamed Minerva. The most important gods were Mars, the god of war; and Jupiter, the king of the gods and god of the light and sky. The Romans also had some original gods called 'indigetes'. Janus, Vesta and Saturn were all indigetes. **FESTIVALS** provided special occasions to honour the gods. The poet Ovid described the rituals of the Paralia festival:

'First sprinkle the ground with water and sweep it with a broom; decorate the sheep-pen with leaves and branches fastened upon it. Make blue smoke from pure sulphur, and let your sheep bleat when she is touched by the smoking sulphur. Burn up the wood of male olive trees, pine and Juniper; and let the laurel singe and crackle in the middle of the hearth. Put a basket of millet with the millet cakes; the country goddess takes special pleasure in this kind of food.'

Mars was the Roman God of War and is usually shown wearing a full suit of armour. This example dates from the 2nd century AD, and was found in Britain.

Source – Ovid, Fasti IV, early-1st century BC

Religion Glossary

altar	Table or flat-topped block used for focus of religious service	**larder**	Cupboard for storing food
		lararium	Place in a house where families would worship
hearth	Area around a fireplace	**sacrifice**	Offering to the gods
indigetes	Gods and goddesses created by the Romans	**shrines**	Holy places for worshipping gods or sacred person

See also: The Roman Army 14–15; Death and Burial 16–17; Living at Home 28–29; Pastimes 30–31

CASE STUDY

The god Mithras was very popular with soldiers because they believed it conquered darkness and disorder. This relief comes from Rome and dates from the 3rd century AD.

The God Mithras

One of the most important gods for the Roman army was Mithras, the god of light and the sun. The sun god Mithras was originally worshipped by the Persians who lived in what is now modern Iran. It reached Rome in the 1st century AD. It appealed to the army because as the god of light, Mithras conquered darkness and disorder. An inscription from Germany shows the dedication of an altar to Mithras:

'In honour of the imperial house, to the unconquerable god Mithras the altar was established as result of a vow to the god at their own expense by Aulus Gratius Iuvenis Father of the rites (of Mithras) and Aulus Gratius Potens, soldier of the XXII legion.'

Source – German inscription, AD 236

9

Writing

There were many different LANGUAGES across the Empire. The Roman writer Cicero believed that better COMMUNICATION within the Empire would help to make people more civilised. Therefore, to help with communication, Latin was used in the west of the Empire and Greek in the east. Language was important for international trade and government. For many of the territories conquered by the Romans, this was the first time that writing was used as a form of communication.

PAPER AND PENS

Tools for writing included a wax tablet with two wooden leaves that folded together.

Liquid wax was poured into the tablet and allowed to harden. The point of the stylus was used like a pen to scratch words into the wax. At the other end of the stylus was a flat end that worked like an eraser – smoothing the wax surface to erase any writing done. Papyrus was a kind of **PAPER** that was made from reeds. It originally came from Egypt. Papyrus was expensive to make and so it was only used for important **DOCUMENTS** like contracts. The **PEN** would have been made from a reed and the ink was a mixture of soot and olive oil. Pliny the Elder describes the making of paper from papyrus:

'... paper is made from the papyrus plant by separating it with a needle point into very thin strips as broad as possible.'

Most writing was done with a wooden wax tablet and bronze stylus and inkwell like these from between 37–68 AD.

Source – Pliny, Natural History, XIII, early-1st century AD

ROMAN ALPHABET

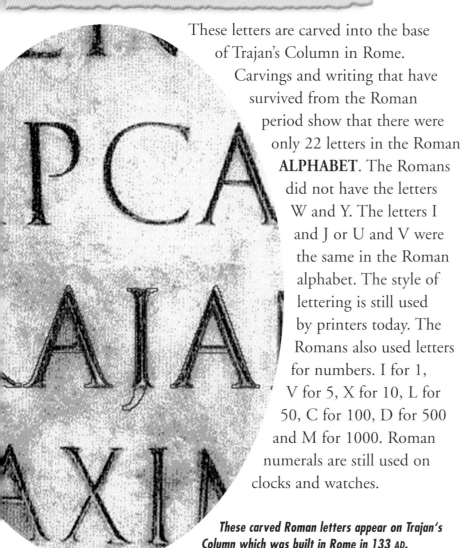

These letters are carved into the base of Trajan's Column in Rome. Carvings and writing that have survived from the Roman period show that there were only 22 letters in the Roman **ALPHABET**. The Romans did not have the letters W and Y. The letters I and J or U and V were the same in the Roman alphabet. The style of lettering is still used by printers today. The Romans also used letters for numbers. I for 1, V for 5, X for 10, L for 50, C for 100, D for 500 and M for 1000. Roman numerals are still used on clocks and watches.

These carved Roman letters appear on Trajan's Column which was built in Rome in 133 AD.

Writing Glossary

broad	*Wide*		*the papyrus plant*
civilised	*Polite and good mannered*	**stylus**	*A writing tool usually*
contract	*Agreements between two*		*made of bronze*
	people put in writing	**territories**	*Areas under the rule of*
Latin	*The language of ancient Rome*		*a single state*
leaves	*Sheets or pages*	**wax tablet**	*Used by Romans to write*
papyrus	*A kind of paper made from*		*on using a stylus*

CASE STUDY

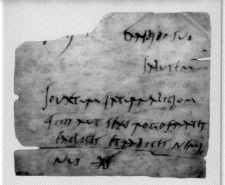

The Vindolanda tablets are letters from people living in northern England in the 1st and 2nd centuries AD.

Writing Letters

The Vindolanda Tablets give a fascinating snapshot of the life of ordinary Romans at the fort of Vindolanda in the north of England. The tablets are made of thinly cut slivers of wood. Letters were written on one side. The wood was then folded in half and the address written on the back. One of the first tablets to be translated says:

'I have sent you … pairs of socks from Sattua, two pairs of sandals and two pairs of underpants … I hope that you live in the greatest good fortune.'

See also: Rulers and Ruled 6–7; Travel and Trade 12–13; Buildings and Engineering 18–19; Dressing Up 26–27

Source – Vindolanda Tablet 346, 1st–2nd century AD

Travel and Trade

The wealth of the Roman Empire aided many regions in building up their production of goods for international trade. The records left by Roman MERCHANTS show that the east of the Empire produced wine, fruit and silk; North Africa produced grain; and Gaul and Spain provided olive oil and wine. The Roman army built many roads which allowed goods to be transported quickly and easily across the Empire.

ROMAN ROADS

The Romans built very straight roads, like this street in Pompeii, Italy.

Roman ROADS are well-known for being extremely straight.

The construction of straight roads was something that emperors would boast about and want to be remembered for. An inscription found next to a road from the reign of Trajan shows this:

'The Emperor Caesar Nerva trajan Augustus Germanicus, son of the deified Nerva, pontifex maximus, holding the tribunician power for the fourth year, father of his country, consul three times, built this road by cutting through mountains and eliminating curves.'

Roman roads were also built to be very strong. So much so that many Roman roads still exist, although they are now under modern road surfaces. Ermine Street originally ran between London and York in England and is now part of a motorway system.

Source – Corpus Inscriptionum Latinarum vol III no,8, c. AD 98–117

Words to use in your project

calculate *(add up)*	**expedition** *(journey)*	**navigate** *(find direction)*
commemorate *(honour the memory of)*	**industry** *(business)*	**trade** *(buying and selling)*
	nautical *(sailing)*	**traverse** *(cross over)*

TRAVELLING BY SEA

The Roman navy patrolled the seas of the Empire, particularly the Mediterranean. **PIRATES** were a real problem for those people who traded by sea. Merchant **SHIPS** often only sailed in the summer months when the weather was safer. The Romans also had no compasses so they made sure they always stayed in sight of land. The writer Synesius wrote this about sea travel:

'For in plain fact the big rollers still kept on, and the sea was at issue with itself. It does this when the wind falls, and the waves it has set going do not fall with it, but, still retaining in full force the impulse that started them, meet the onset of the gale, and to its front oppose their own. Well, when people are sailing in such circumstances, life hangs, as they say, by a slender thread.'

Sailing was dangerous in Roman times because of pirates and crude equipment. This relief of a sailing ship comes from Italy and dates from the 3rd century AD.

Source – Synesius, letter to his brother, c. late-3rd–early 4th centuries AD

Travel and Trade Glossary

deified	Worshipped as a god	**steelyard**	Part of a machine used for weighing
eliminating	Getting rid of something		
gale	Gusty wind	**tribunician**	Roman official chosen by the people to protect their interests
impulse	Sudden urge		
retaining	Keeping		
rollers	Part of a vehicle that helps it to move	**uncia**	The basic unit of weight in Roman times

CASE STUDY

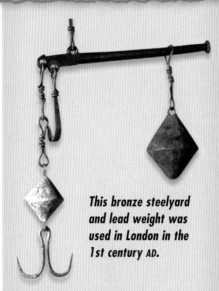

This bronze steelyard and lead weight was used in London in the 1st century AD.

Weighing and Measuring

Trade became easier when the Romans standardised rules about **MEASURING** across the whole Empire. This meant that merchants from the furthest parts of the Empire could **BUY AND SELL** from each other knowing that the way of measuring was the same everywhere. The basic unit of weight in the Roman Empire was the uncia (where we get our word for ounce). An uncia was about 27 grams. The steelyard and weight was one of the most common ways of **WEIGHING** goods. The Romans sometimes used their denarius coin as a measure of weight. Around 155 BC–AD 64 the denarius weighed 1/7 ounce, as described by the writer, Celsus:

'... in the ounce there is a weight of 7 denarii'.

Source – Celsus, On Medicine, V.17.1.C, mid-1st century AD

See also: Writing 10–11; Buildings and Engineering 18–19; Food and Drink 24–25; Dressing Up 26–27

The Roman Army

Life in the Roman Army was tough. Soldiers were KILLED for sleeping while they were supposed to be keeping guard. For cowardice, a unit was decimated. Yet many still rushed to join the army. Not only did it pay quite well, but it was a chance to learn new SKILLS. After retirement, soldiers were given land and money. This meant that soldiers who were not Roman citizens were given rights and privileges they would not have had otherwise.

WEAPONS

The ordinary soldier had a spear called a 'pilum', a dagger called a 'pugio' and a short sword called a 'gladius'. They were also well protected by metal armour.

These **WEAPONS** made Roman soldiers very effective in battle. The Romans also had huge battering rams, stone-throwing machines and a big crossbow that could fire bolts at **ENEMY** walls. A writer from the period described the Roman weaponry:

'The legion in practice is victorious because of the number of soldiers and the type of machines. First of all, it is equipped with hurling machines which no breastplate, no shield can withstand. For the practice is to have a ballista mounted on a carriage for each century, to each of which are assigned mules and a team of eleven men for loading and firing.'

Trajan's Column was erected in Rome to honour Emperor Trajan and features scenes from the battles he fought in Dacia (modern Romania) between AD 101 and 106. It stands 30 metres high.

Source – Vegetius, Military Science II.23, c. early-5th century AD

Words to use in your project

| battlefield (piece of ground where battle is fought) exec/ executed (killed as | punishment) formidable (big and impressive) | legionnaire (foot soldier) centurion (soldier who is higher up than legionnaire) |

PEOPLE IN THE ARMY

The army was organised into legions. Each legion had about 10,000 men. The ordinary foot **SOLDIER** was called a legionnaire. Above the legionnaire was the centurion. The centurion had heavier armour and his helmet had a red plume, so he was easily recognised. Many soldiers were critical of their superiors. This is illustrated in the following account of a **MUTINY** among the legions stationed at the Northern border of the empire in the first century AD:

'Why should they obey like slaves a few centurions and fewer tribunes, when old men, and many who had lost limbs from wounds, were serving thirty and fourty years?'

This Roman centurion is from a 2nd century relief from Turin, Italy.

Source – Tacitus Annals I. xvii, late-1st century BC

The Roman Army Glossary

cowardice	Lacking courage
customarily	Most commonly
decimated	When one out of ten soldiers was executed
entailing	Involving
fort	Area for defending against an attack
mutiny	Rebellion against the authorities
privileges	Special rights and honours
rampart	A defensive wall

CASE STUDY

This Roman fort was built between AD 120–138 in Cumbria, England.

Walls of Defence

Soldiers spent their winter months or times of peace in **FORTS**. A typical fort held between 500–1,000 troops. Every fort was defended by a ditch, a rampart and a high stone **WALL**. In the centre of each fort was the 'principia' or headquarters of the fort. Here is a quote from the Emperor Hadrian praising an army legion's wall-building skills:

'You have built a wall entailing long labour, such as is customarily made for permanent winter quarters ... built of large heavy stones of all sizes ... You have cut a trench straight through hard coarse gravel and have made it even by smoothing it.'

Source – Excerpt from Hadrian's address to a legion based in North Africa, AD 128

See also: Creation of the Roman Empire 4–5; Rulers and Ruled 6–7; Travel and Trade 12–13; Buildings and Engineering 18–19

Death and Burial

During the Roman Empire, people did not have modern MEDICINES, their diet was not very healthy and their living conditions were hard. This meant that many people did not live to reach 50 years old. Many children died at birth or caught DISEASES that they could not fight off. Therefore, the Romans were familiar with death. Because it was so much a part of their lives, they created all sorts of RITUALS to go with the funeral and burial of a loved one.

CEMETERIES

This cemetery in Pompeii, Italy has many grand tombs that contain the remains of wealthy Romans.

In about 450 BC Roman law ruled that the dead were not allowed to be buried inside the city walls. It stated that:

'None is to bury or burn a corpse in the city.'

This was done for religious reasons but also had a practical use as it prevented the spread of disease in the tightly-packed streets of Roman towns. **CEMETERIES** were built near the town gates. The richest Romans were buried in tombs along the roadside. People travelling along the road could then see the tombs and remember those who were inside. Poorer people could pay for the ashes of relatives to be placed in small spaces in special buildings. The bodies of the poorest members of Roman society and slaves were simply thrown together into large pits and buried without any ceremony.

Source – Twelve Tables, Table X.1

THE FUNERAL

This Roman urn from the 1st century AD was made for the ashes of a young woman, honouring her marriage.

Early on in the Roman Empire, cremation of the dead body was common. A cinerary urn was used to deposit the ashes of the dead. It would then be placed in a family **TOMB** or in a cemetery. Later, Romans began to bury their dead. Provided there was enough money, the **FUNERAL** would take place within two days and would usually happen in the evening. A Roman writer wrote about the funeral of a rich Roman:

'After this, when the burial and the usual rituals have been carried out they place the image of the dead man in the most conspicuous place in the house, enclosed in a wooded shrine. This image consists of a mask that reproduces his features and complexion with remarkable faithfulness.'

Source – Polybius, Histories 53-4.3, 2nd century BC

CASE STUDY

This coffin detail from about AD 150–180 shows the god Hercules at the gates of the Underworld.

The River Styx

Throughout the period of the Roman Empire, there were many different ideas about death. Many believed in an **AFTERLIFE**. Inscriptions on tombstones show that the Romans believed that the dead would be ferried across the Styx, a river that led to the underworld. A coin was often placed in the mouth of the body so that the ferryman could be paid. Here the process is described:

'The ferryman there is Charon. Those sailing the waters of the Styx have all been buried. No man may be ferried from fearful bank to fearful bank of this roaring current until his bones are laid to rest.'

Virgil, Aeneid, late-1st century BC

Death and Burial Glossary

cinerary urn	Container for storing dead person's ashes	**River Styx**	The river used by the ferryman to transport the dead to the underworld
complexion	Tone and texture of skin		
conspicuous	Very obvious	**tomb**	Structure where rich person is buried
cremation	Burning a dead body before burying or scattering the ashes	**underworld**	Place where the dead gather under the earth

See also: Rulers and Ruled 6–7; Religion 8–9; Travel and Trade 12–13; Health 22–23

Buildings and Engineering

The Romans copied many building styles from the Greeks, particularly large, important buildings like STADIUMS or temples. The Romans were the first to use domes on top of their buildings. They were also the first to use a lot of arches on their structures. Whenever the Romans built within the Empire they used local materials. For larger buildings they brought in marble from Greece or Italy. The Romans were also the first to use CONCRETE for building.

BUILDING TOOLS

Roman BUILDERS used dividers when they worked with models or drawings of the structure that they were building.

If large blocks of stone had to be placed together on a building or a bridge, it was essential that the blocks fitted together well. The Romans use a set square to check on this. A plumb bob would have been used to make sure that vertical lines were straight. Good engineering depended on accurate **MEASUREMENTS**. The Romans made measurements of length the same across the Empire so that there would be no confusion. The ruler is divided into the basic unit of length, the digitus. The digitus is about 18 mm. There are 16 of these in a Pes and 5 Pes makes a Passus. A Roman mile was about 1,000 Passus.

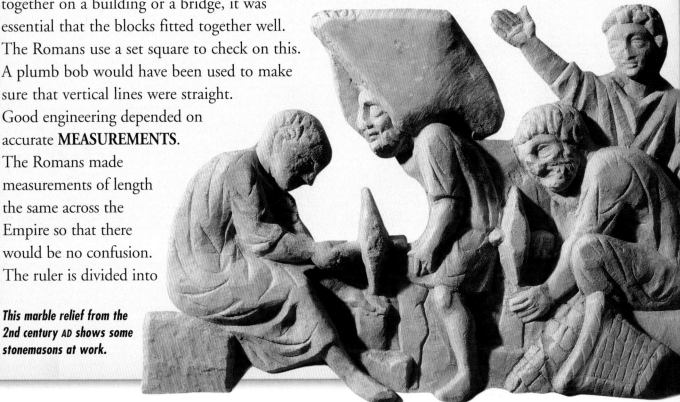

This marble relief from the 2nd century AD shows some stonemasons at work.

Words to use in your project

frontier *(border)*	legacy *(something passed on to people)*
implements *(tools)*	
irrigation *(water supply)*	structures *(buildings)*
technology *(way things work)*	
pozzolana *(the Roman name for concrete)*	

CARRYING WATER

The Pont du Gard aqueduct in Nimes, Southern France was built in the 1st century BC.

The job of an aqueduct was to provide a city with a **WATER SUPPLY**. The water would flow along a covered channel at the top of the structure. The invention of the aqueduct shows that the Romans did not build grand buildings just to show off – they also had a practical purpose. The importance of aqueducts to Rome is described in the following quote:

'... they are structures of the greatest magnitude, and ... each one carries several conduits; for should it once be necessary to interrupt these, the City would be deprived of the greater part of its water-supply.'

Source – Frontinus, The Water Supply of Rome II, late-1st century AD

Buildings and Engineering Glossary

aqueduct	A bridge designed for carrying water	**engineering**	Designing and building things
conduits	Channels for water to flow through	**fort**	Strong building or position used for warfare
deprived	Lacking something	**magnitude**	Great size or importance
digitus	The basic unit of measuring length in the Roman Empire	**marauding**	Attacking and stealing
		mortar	Building material for holding bricks together

CASE STUDY

Hadrian's Wall

In 122 AD, Emperor Hadrian ordered that a wall be built across northern England to mark the border of the Empire and to keep out marauding northern tribes. Modern historians believe it took Roman soldiers between six and eight years to build. It runs for about 120 kilometres. The wall was originally built of earth and wood but was gradually strengthened to a stone wall about 10 metres high and two to three metres thick. The stone wall was made from locally available materials such as rubble, mortar and stone. To further strengthen the defences, there were **FORTS** every thousand paces along the whole length of the wall. In its completed form the wall was an impressive monument.

This is a view of Hadrian's Wall in northern England which was built in the 2nd century AD.

See also: Travel and Trade 12–13; The Roman Army 14–15; Health 22–23; Living at Home 28–29

Gladiators

The gladiatorial contest was a FIGHT between two men in front of a huge crowd, from which only one would survive. People today often consider it the most barbaric of Roman customs, although in Roman times they were very popular events. It is believed that gladiatorial contests began as part of a ceremony at the funerals of important people like WARRIORS. However, by the time of the emperors, the contest had simply become a spectacle for enjoyment.

GLADIATOR FIGHTS

Gladiators were trained in special schools called 'ludi'. They were often slaves and criminals, although many Romans actually chose to become gladiators.

If a gladiator survived many fights, he was regarded as a **HERO** and might become famous. At the end of the gladiatorial fight, the crowd decided whether the loser should live. If the fight took place in front of the Emperor, then the final decision was his. Pliny the Younger described the glory of being a gladiator:

'Next came a public entertainment – nothing lax or dissolute to weaken and destroy the manly spirit of his subjects, but one to inspire them to face honourable wounds and look scorn on death, be exhibiting love of glory and desire for victory.'

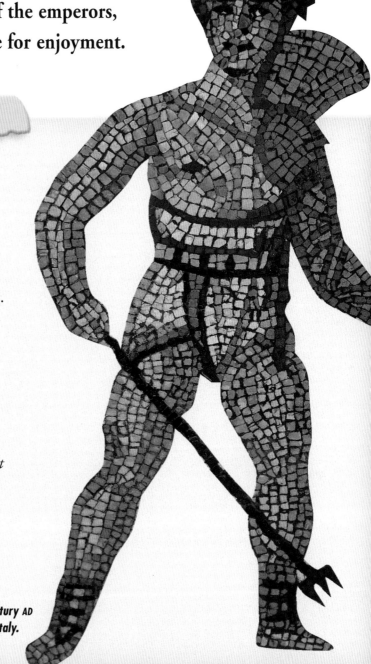

This image of a gladiator comes from a 1st century AD Roman mosaic, from a Roman villa in Italy.

Source – Pliny the Younger, Panegyric, AD 100

COLOSSEUM

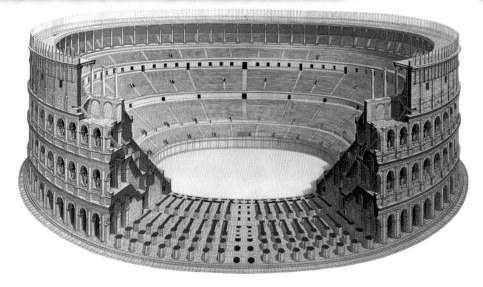

Rome's Colosseum was finished in AD 80 and was used to stage gladiatorial contests.

The most spectacular place for gladiatorial contests was the **COLOSSEUM** in Rome which was completed in AD 80. It could hold over 50,000 people at one time. Enough of the Colosseum still remains for us to see what it first looked like. An awning could be stretched across the top to give shade to the onlookers.

Below this were cells where the gladiators were kept before being led out to fight. The arena was covered with sand, which would absorb the **BLOOD** and be swept away easily. A Roman writer describes how:

'... at the dedication of the Colosseum, Titus provided a most lavish gladiatorial show.'

Source – Suetonius, Life of Titus, VII.3, 1st half of the 2nd century AD

Gladiators Glossary

awning	A sheet of canvas stretched over a frame	**ludi**	Special schools were gladiators were trained
deflect	Shield from a blow	**retiarius**	A lightly armoured gladiator
exposed	In full view	**secutor**	A heavily armoured gladiator
lavish	Fancy and expensive	**trident**	A special spear with three points at the end
lax	Not very strict		

CASE STUDY

Gladiator's Gear

There were two types of gladiators – the 'secutor' and the 'retiarus'. The **ARMOUR** worn by the secutor gave some protection during the fight, but the weight of the armour could also slow him down as well. Meanwhile, the 'retiarus' had only a short tunic to wear. This meant that he was unprotected but was much quicker. The retiarus also had a net that he used to try and catch his opponent and a trident to stab him. A Roman writer named Seneca described a contest between two lightly armed gladiators:

'The men have no defensive armour. They are exposed to blows at all points, and no one ever strikes in vain ... there is no helmet or shield to deflect the weapon.'

*A secutor would have worn a **HELMET** like this one from Pompeii, Italy, 1st century AD.*

Source – Suetonius, Life of Titus, VII.3, 1st half of the 2nd century AD

See also: Rulers and Ruled 6–7; Buildings and Engineering 18–19; Dressing Up 26–27; Pastimes 30–31

Health

Many Romans believed that ILLNESSES were caused by curses, WITCHCRAFT or punishment from the gods. Therefore, many of them looked to the supernatural for their cures. Praying at shrines, carrying charms and leaving offerings to the gods were all supposed to help CURE an illness. If medicines were used then they were usually herbs with healing properties. The Romans learnt about the importance of keeping clean from the Greeks.

ROMAN TOILETS

The Romans developed a water-supply system which helped to prevent many diseases.

TOILETS were communal and used as places to meet and talk. Underneath the toilets, a stream of water carried away waste. People would then clean themselves with a sponge soaked in vinegar on a stick. Vinegar would have killed off GERMS. The sponge was then cleaned in a small stream that ran in front of the toilets. The Romans took great care of their sewers. In 33 BC, Emperor Augustus' right-hand man, Agrippa:

'... cleaned out the sewers, and sailed underground through them to the Tiber'.

Roman toilets such as these from Housesteads Fort on Hadrian's Wall were built so that a stream of running water could wash away the waste.

Source – Cassius Dio, History, 49.43.1-4, 3rd century AD

Words to use in your project

administer (give something)	**communal** (together)	**hygiene** (keeping clean)
amputation (have a limb cut off)	**grooming** (looking after your appearance)	**sophisticated** (advanced)
		talisman (powerful charm)

DOCTORS

The Romans had no proper anesthetics so any operations must have been agony. They did not have any antiseptics either so wounds became infected, often leading to amputation or even death.

DOCTORS tried to heal their patients with many different kinds of **HERBS**, such as fenugreek for pneumonia and peppermint for stomach trouble.

The Emperor Marcus Aurelius had a doctor called Galen who wrote about all sorts of medical subjects:

'About Marcus Aurelius I know personally that for his own safety he used to prepare and take each day as much as an Egyptian bean's worth (a small measure) of this antidote, swallowing this either with or without admixture of water or wine or the like. And when he began to get very drowsy at his daily occupations, he took away the poppy-juice.'

This 1st century BC picture from Pompeii, Italy shows a warrior named Aeneas having an arrow-head removed from his leg by a surgeon.

Source – Galen, Antidotes 1.1, mid-2nd century AD

Health Glossary

anaesthetic	A drug given to take away the pain before an operation	**chatelaine**	Small collection of things pinned to clothing
antidote	Cure	**communal**	All in together
antiseptics	Mixture that prevents germs getting in	**drowsy**	Tired
		luxurious	Very comfortable
capacious	A lot of space inside	**supernatural**	Caused by God

CASE STUDY

This Roman châtelaine was pinned to clothing and used for keeping fingernails clean and so forth.

Keeping Clean

Personal hygiene was important to the ancient Romans. Many Romans pinned a chatelaine of cleaning implements to their clothing. This included tweezers, a fingernail cleaner and an ear cleaner. Visits to the public baths in order to wash was a regular feature in the lives of Romans. Wealthy people took their slaves with them to the baths to assist them in washing. Lucian, writing in the 2nd century AD describes a luxurious **BATHING** complex:

'... capacious locker rooms to undress in on each side, with a very high and brilliantly lighted hall in between them, in which are three swimming pools of cold water; it is finished in Laconian marble ...'

Source – Lucian, The Bath, 2nd century AD

Food and Drink

The Romans enjoyed their food. Most Romans ate very little during the day and had their largest meal in the evening. For poor Romans their DIET was mostly bread, lentils and a small piece of meat. It was fashionable to add lots of HERBS AND SPICES to food, especially as the food was not always that fresh. One of the most popular sauces was garum, which was a strong-tasting fish sauce.

HOW THEY COOKED FOOD

The central hearth was heated using wood or charcoal. Several of the emperors, including Julius Caesar, were worried about the risk of fire in their cities so didn't allow the use of OVENS in the home.

Poorer Romans would not have been able to afford an oven even if they were allowed them. They relied on buying hot food from bars called thermapholia which could be found on many Roman city streets.
The Roman writer Seneca described them:

'... the varied cries of the sausage dealer and confectioner and of all the peddlers of the cook shops, hawking their wares, each with his own peculiar intonation.'

Cooking was usually done in **SAUCEPANS** made of bronze because they cooked the food more evenly.

This stone oven is preserved in the city of Pompeii in Italy.

Source – Seneca, Moral Letter 41.2, mid-1st century AD

Words to use in your project

banquet *(feast)*
condiments *(something for flavouring food)*

culinary *(cooking)*
dilute *(added water)*
etiquette *(polite behaviour)*

indulged *(enjoyed or satisfied)*
lavish *(generous)*
neat *(no water added)*

DRINKS

Wealthy Romans drank from glass drinking **CUPS**, while ordinary Romans used pottery cups. Most Romans drank wine. It was considered bad manners to drink **WINE** with no water added. They also added flavours like herbs and honey. In a letter, Pliny the Younger described how a dinner host gave different qualities of wine to different guests:

'He had even put the wine into tiny little flasks, divided into three categories, not with the idea of giving his guests the opportunity of choosing, but to make it impossible for them to refuse what they were given. One lot was intended for himself and for us, another for his lesser friends (all his friends are graded) and the third for his and our freedmen.'

This glass drinking vessel from the 4th century BC would have been used by wealthy Romans.

Source – Seneca, Moral Letter 41.2, mid-1st century AD

Food and Drink Glossary

confectioner	*Person who sells sweets*	**intonation**	*The rise and fall of the voice when speaking*
flasks	*Containers for liquid*		
garum	*Fish sauce*	**peddlers**	*Salesmen*
Gaul	*Ancient name for modern-day France*	**thermopolia**	*Popular bars where many Romans bought hot meals*
hawking	*Selling goods in the streets*	**unique**	*Special or original*

See also: Travel and Trade 12–13; Death and Burial 16–17; Health 22–23; Living at Home 28–29

CASE STUDY

This Samian ware plate from the 3rd century AD was very fashionable in ancient Rome.

Bowls and Plates

Rich Romans wanted to eat their food off the most fashionable **BOWLS** and **PLATES**. In the 1st and 2nd centuries AD, it was a glossy red pottery called Samian ware that would have been used by the most fashion-conscious Romans. Samian ware was made in large factories in Italy and Gaul and was sent to every corner of the Roman Empire and beyond as well. A 1st century writer named Petronius mocked a rich man who boasted about the quality of his plate and glass ware:

'Perhaps you're wondering why I am unique in owning Corinthian plates? Because, of course, the dealer I buy it from is named Corinthus.'

Source – Pliny the Younger, Letters, II.6, early-2nd century AD

Dressing Up

Not only did the Romans care about the CLOTHES they wore but they also made sure that they had the best jewellery, HAIRSTYLES and make-up. Roman children did not have their own fashions and simply wore smaller versions of their parents' clothes. Fashions changed throughout the Roman Empire. For instance, in the early years of the Empire, Roman men had long hair and curly beards. By the end of the Roman Empire the fashion was to be clean-shaven and to have short hair.

THE CLOTHES THEY WORE

All Roman citizens had the right to wear a toga but these were only worn on special occasions. For everyday wear both men and women wore light tunics.

Both **TOGAS** and tunics were large single pieces of cloth that were fastened at the shoulder with a brooch or pin. Light colours – especially white – were the most popular. Trousers were considered fit to be worn only by barbarians and foreigners. On their feet, both men and women wore sandals. When a state was conquered by the Romans, the people often adopted the Roman style of dress. This illustrated the widespread influence of Roman ideas. Tacitus, in his account of his Father in Law Agricola's governorship of Britain described this:

'... *even our style of dress came in to favour and the toga was everywhere to be seen [in Britain].*'

This funerary mosaic from the 1st century BC shows a man wearning a white toga. The toga was worn on special occasions.

Source – Tacitus Agricola 21, AD 97-8

ROMAN JEWELLERY

Women wore a lot of jewellery. The Romans originally followed the Greek example of putting gemstones into their **RINGS** and **BRACELETS**. The Romans took this idea further, adding different kinds of stones and pearls. Both men and women wore rings and sometimes had them on all ten fingers. The wealthiest Romans also wore cameos set into rings and pendants. The cameo normally showed people, gods or mythological figures. The poet Juvenal, who didn't like women very much, wrote about the way women dress up in jewellery:

'There is nothing that a woman will not permit herself to do, nothing that she deems shameful, when she encircles her neck with green emeralds, and fastens huge pearls to her elongated ears: there is nothing more intolerable than a wealthy woman.'

This pure gold amulet from the 1st century AD was found in Pompeii, Italy.

> Source – Juvenal, Satire VI, late-1st–early-2nd century AD

Dressing Up Glossary

cameo	A picture made of one material and placed on top of another material	intolerable	Unpleasant
		ochre	A pale brown or yellow mineral made of clay
complexion	Colour and condition of skin	sediment	Bits that settle at the bottom of liquid
elongated	Stretched		
funerary		toga	Loose flowing piece of clothing
mosaic	Artwork made to honour someone who has died	tunic	A piece of clothing made of thin material without sleeves and reaching to the knee

See also: Creation of the Empire 4–5; Writing 10–11; Travel and Trade 12–13; Gladiators 20–21

CASE STUDY

This small make-up grinder was found by a metal detector in Britain in the 1st century AD.

Make-up Grinder

MAKE-UP grinders were used to grind up minerals to use as make-up. Rich Roman women used make-up whenever they were going out in public. It was fashionable to have a pale complexion. This showed that they did not have to go outdoors to work. Many women applied make-up to make themselves look more pale. This was normally made of chalk or white lead, which was very poisonous. Cheeks and lips were coloured red using ochre or the sediment from red wine. The eybrows and edges of the eyes were normally made black with ash. Make-up was stored in small pots and bottles.

Living at Home

Most Roman HOUSES were small and low-quality. In towns and cities, people lived in crowded flats called tenements. These were several stories high and had no running water or sanitation. We know more about town houses than country houses because several emperors were worried about the condition of the tenements and passed laws to try and limit their height. Wealthier Romans could afford to have both a TOWN house and a villa in the COUNTRY.

ROMAN HOUSES

Most Roman villas followed the same design. The first room that a visitor would walk into would be the hallway or 'atrium'.

The atrium had an opening in the roof and a pool. This was meant to help keep the house cool in summer. Frescoes from the Roman period show us that the Romans preferred their rooms to have little in the way of **FURNITURE**, but they did like to have rich decorations on the walls and floor. In other parts of the Roman Empire villas varied and copied local tastes. Early villas in Britain were usually a line of rooms with a colonnade at the front. The younger Pliny boasts to a friend of 'the charm of his Laurentine villa' in Italy, saying that:

'... the villa is spacious enough for my needs, and the upkeep is not expensive'.

This is a view from the outside of a Roman villa in Herculaneum, Italy.

Source – Pliny the Younger, letter to his friend, late-1st–early-2nd century AD

DECORATING THE HOUSE

The **FLOORS** of wealthy Romans were decorated with mosaics. This form of home decoration was practised in Egypt in the 3rd century BC and was adopted by the Romans. Many mosaics have survived because they were very strong once they were set in place. The scenes on mosaics were normally taken from legends or daily life. Along with the floors, the interior **WALLS** of villas were often decorated with frescoes. These normally featured pictures from myths. Rich Romans also had outdoor scenes painted on to the walls so that they looked like views from the window.

This wall mosaic of a man drinking is from the 1st century AD. Villa mosaics often showed scenes from daily life.

Living at Home Glossary

atrium	The hallway inside a Roman villa		heating
colonnade	A line of columns	mosaic	Pictures created on floors using small pieces of tile
fresco	A painting done on a wall while the plaster is still wet	sanitation	Public health
		tenements	Block of flats
hypocaust	A kind of underfloor central	villa	A house owned by a wealthy Roman

See also: Religion 8–9; Buildings and Engineering 18–19; Food and Drink 24–25; Pastimes 30–31

CASE STUDY

This hypocaust from the 1st century BC is from the Gallo-Roman town of Alesia in France.

Keeping Warm

Villas in the northern parts of the Roman Empire needed to be kept warm. To do this, they used an underfloor **CENTRAL-HEATING** system called a 'hypocaust'. A fire was lit next to an outside wall and was kept going by a slave. The heat would be drawn into an open space under the floor and the heat would then rise through the floor into the walls. In some villas the heat passed through holes in the wall as well. These hypocausts can be seen in many Roman buildings, particularly in Pompeii. Pliny described the use of heating to keep his villa warm:

'Attached to this is a bedroom connected to a passageway with a hollow floor and walls fitted with pipes from which it receives hot air circulated in all directions at a healthful temperature.'

Source – Pliny, Letter, II. 17, late-1st–early 2nd century AD

Pastimes

Every Roman, with the exception of slaves, was given many HOLIDAYS. Originally, these were days that celebrated religious festivals. Over time, the activities that went with these festivals lost their religious meaning and became pure ENTERTAINMENT. In the reign of Claudius, 159 days a year were declared as public holidays. By the middle of the 5th century AD, this had risen to 200 holidays a year. Enjoying their spare time was an important part of Roman life.

THEATRE

Many Roman towns had an open-air theatre. These were usually semi-circular in shape.

The audience sat on the curved sides of the **THEATRE** facing a raised stage. The plays that were performed were either Greek plays that were translated into Latin or were written by Romans in the Greek style. Roman theatre-goers preferred comedies. The Romans also invented two new forms of theatre. They were the first people to use mime and pantomime. The importance of theatre and entertainment is illustrated by the following quote from an early imperial Roman writer:

'..it was the height of political wisdom for the emperor not to neglect even actors and other performers of the stage, circus and the arena, since he knew that the Roman people is held fast by two things above all, the grain supply and the theatrical shows.'

This mosaic of a tragic theatre mask was created in the 1st century AD.

Source – Fronto, Elements of History, XVII, 2nd century AD

Words to use in your project

corruption (bad behaviour)	*play music*)	**popular** (liked by many people)
festivities (fun celebrations)	**patron** (person or figure	**vulgar** (lacking class or
performance (act or	who is a symbol for something)	good taste)

PUBLIC BATHS

The public baths, such as this one in the English city of Bath, were popular places to spend leisure time.

As well as for keeping clean, the Romans went to the public baths to meet friends, **EXERCISE** with weights or to play ball games. For those with less energy there were board **GAMES** and marbles. The Roman writer, Seneca, who lived above some baths, gave a useful description:

'When the stronger fellows are exercising and swinging heavy laden weights in their hands, when they are working hard or pretending to be working hard, I hear their groans ... Add to this the arrest of a brawler or a thief, and the fellow who always likes to hear his own voice in the bath, and those who jump into the pool with a mighty splash as they strike the water.'

Source – Seneca, Moral Letter 41.1-2, mid-1st century AD

Pastimes Glossary

abide	*Put up with*	**lyre**	*Popular stringed instrument that was plucked like a harp*
brawler	*Someone who is in a fight*		
corruption	*Acting dishonestly for money or personal gain*	**pantomime**	*Piece of drama or poetry with music and dance*
dregs	*Most worthless parts*	**pastimes**	*Hobbies and activities people do in their spare time*
fraction	*Part of a whole*		
lingo	*Language*	**semi-circular**	*Half of a circle*

See also: Religion 8–9; Gladiators 20–21; Health 22–23; Living at Home 28–29

CASE STUDY

The God of Music

According to Roman mythology, the god Apollo would entertain the other gods with **MUSIC** and poetry. For this reason, Apollo was seen as the patron of music. For wealthy Romans music was seen as something that was beneath them. For instance, the Roman writer, Juvenal complained that listening or **DANCING** to music could lead to corruption largely because they were associated with Greek luxury. As Juvenal says:

'I cannot abide a Rome of Greeks; and yet what fraction of our dregs comes from Greece? The Syrian Orontes has long since poured into the Tiber, bringing with it its lingo and its manners, its flutes and its slanting harp-strings.'

However, music was popular with most people. Instruments included the lyre and many types of wind instrument.

This 2nd century AD statue of the Roman god of music, Apollo, is from Cyrene in Libya.

Source – Juvenal, Satire III. 58, late-1st–early 2nd AD

Index

ANCIENT ROME TIMELINE

753 BC
The city of Rome is founded by Romulus and Remus (according to Roman mythology).

509 BC
The Republic of Rome is established after the Etruscans are driven out.

450 BC
The Romans establish their first written laws called the Twelve Tables.

390 BC
The Gauls invade Italy and are defeated by the Romans.

300–400 BC
The Romans are exposed to Greek ideas. They begin to worship Greek gods and goddesses, but they gave them Roman names.

140s BC
Rome gains control of North Africa, Spain, Greece, Macedonia and part of Turkey.

60s BC
Rome conquers eastern Asia Minor, Syria, and Judea under the direction of general Pompey.

58–51 BC
Julius Caesar conquers Gaul (modern France).

49 BC
Caesar invades Italy, starting a civil war.

44 BC
Caesar is assassinated by a group of senators who hope to restore

the Roman Republic. Civil war breaks out again.

43 BC
Mark Antony fights for control of Rome – seeking help from Cleopatra, queen of Egypt. They fall in love.

30 BC
Rome conquers Egypt.

27 BC
Augustus becomes the first emporer of Rome. His rule marks the period we know as Pax Romana (Roman Peace). It lasted for about 200 years.

AD 30
Jesus Christ was crucified by the Romans for treason. However, his followers begin to spread Christianity throughout the Roman Empire.

AD 43
Emperor Claudius invades Britain.

AD 200s
The Goths, a Germanic tribe, invade the Roman Empire on numerous occasions.

Late AD 300s
Christianity becomes the official religion of the empire.

Early AD 400s
Germanic tribes invade Spain, Gaul (now France), and northern Africa

AD 410
The Visigoths invade and loot Rome.

AD 476
The Last Roman Emperor is overthrown.

PICTURE CREDITS: Alamy: 31t. **Art Archive:** 4-5ct, 7tl, 8bl, 8-9c, 10b, 11tl, 14bl, 14-15c, 15tr, 15tl, 18r, 19tl, 20r, 22l, 22-23c, 24-25ct, 25tr, 26cb, 28-29ct, 29tr, 30c. **Bridgeman Art Library:** 7tr, 11tr, 13tr. **British Museum:** 6c, 17l, 17tr, 23tr, 27tr, 31br. **Corbis:** 9tr, 12bl, 16cl, 24bl, 27tl. **Heritage Images:** 19cr, 21br, 28bl. **Scala Archives:** 12-13ct. **Werner Forman:** 5tr.